WHAT IS SOIL AND WHY IS IT IMPORTANT?

2nd Grade Science Workbook

Children's Earth Sciences Books Edition

SPEEDY
PUBLISHING

Speedy Publishing LLC
40 E. Main St. #1156
Newark, DE 19711
www.speedypublishing.com

Soil is more than
just the dirt.

Soil is one of Earth's most precious resources.

Soil is formed as rock is broken up by ice, frost, wind, and water.

Soil consists of crumbling rock or sand, clay, dead plant and animal remains, fungi and even manure.

Soil also contains lots of tiny creatures, such as earthworms.

Earthworms turn the plant and animal material into nutrients.

There are three main types of soil-clay, sandy, and loamy.

Soil is divided into layers from the surface down to the underlying bedrock. This is called a soil profile.

It takes more than 500 years to form two centimeters of topsoil.

There are more micro-organisms in a handful of soil than there are people on earth.

Soil acts as a filter for underground water, filtering out pollutants.

Soils modify the atmosphere by emitting and absorbing gases.

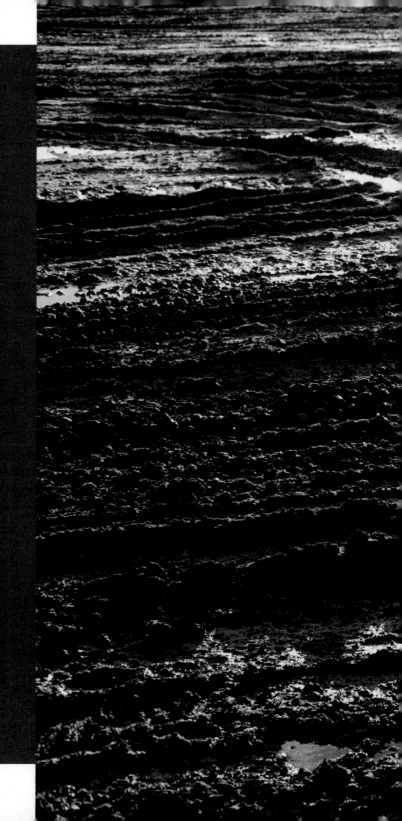

Soil consists of 45% minerals, 25% water, 25% air & 5% organic matter.

Soils process recycled nutrients, including carbon, so that living things can use them over and over again.

Soils serve as engineering media for construction of foundations, dams and buildings.

Soil is where the plants grow.

Farmers need healthy soil to grow crops and feed people.

Only 25 percent of the earth's surface is made up of soil and only 10 percent of that soil can be used to grow food.

Soil is at the bottom of the food chain, yet it is the cornerstone of life on earth.